Books should be returned on or bef
last date stamped below.

D0590864

Space Observer
THE MOON

Jenny Tesar

First published in Great Britain by Heinemann Library
Halley Court, Jordan Hill, Oxford OX2 8EJ
a division of Reed Educational and Professional Publishing Ltd.

Heinemann is a registered trademark of Reed Educational & Professional Publishing Limited.

OXFORD MELBOURNE AUCKLAND
JOHANNESBURG BLANTYRE GABORONE
IBADAN PORTSMOUTH NH CHICAGO

Designed by AMR and Celia Floyd
Originated by Dot Gradations Ltd
Printed and bound in Hong Kong/China

04 03 02 01 00
10 9 8 7 6 5 4 3 2 1

ISBN 0 431 01440 X

British Library Cataloguing in Publication Data

Tesar, Jenny
  The moon. – (Space observer) (Take-off!)
  1. Moon – Juvenile literature
  I. Title
  523.3

J523.3
1174018

Acknowledgements

The publishers would like to thank the following for permission to reproduce photographs:
Pages 4–5: ©Galen Rowell/Peter Arnold, Inc.; pages 6, 7, 8, and 18: Gazelle Technologies, Inc.; pages 9, 10–11: ©NASA/Peter Arnold, Inc.; page 12: ©Ted Clutter/Photo Researchers, Inc.; page 13: ©Jeff Greenberg/MRP/Photo Researchers, Inc.; pages 14–15, 16: ©John Bova/Photo Researchers, Inc.; page 17: ©Francois Gohier/Photo Researchers, Inc.; page 19: ©NASA/Science Source/Photo Researchers, Inc.; pages 20–21: ©Julian Baum/Science Photo Library/Photo Researchers, Inc.; pages 22–23: PhotoDisc, Inc.

Cover photograph: OSF/Robert Comport

The Publishers would like to thank Sue Graves for her advice and expertise in the preparation of this book.

Every effort has been made to contact copyright holders of any material reproduced in this book.
Any omissions will be rectified in subsequent printings if notice is given to the Publisher.

For more information about Heinemann Library books, or to order, please telephone +44(0)1865 888066, or send a fax to +44(0)1865 314091. You can visit our website at www.heinemann.co.uk

Any words appearing in bold, **like this**, are explained in the Glossary.

Contents

What is the Moon?

The Moon is a big, round ball of rock. It is Earth's nearest neighbour. It is more than 384,000 kilometres from Earth.

The Moon travels around the Earth in a big oval path called an **orbit**. At the same time, the Earth orbits around the Sun. The Moon is called a **satellite** of the **planet** Earth. This means that the Moon travels around the Earth.

If you could drive from Earth to the Moon in a car, it would take 200 days to get there!

How big is the Moon?

From Earth, the Moon looks as big as the Sun. But the Sun is about 400 times wider than the Moon. The Moon looks the same size because it is much closer to Earth.

From Earth, the Moon looks as big as the Sun.

This picture shows what Earth looks like from the Moon's **surface**.

The Moon is also smaller than Earth. Earth is about four times bigger than the Moon.

Some scientists think the Moon was once a part of the Earth.

The Moon's surface

The Moon's **surface** has dark and bright areas. The dark areas are smooth and flat. They are **plains**. The bright areas are rough. They are mountains and **craters**.

There are mountains and craters on the Moon.

The Moon's craters were made by rocks crashing into its surface.

Craters are holes in the Moon's surface. Most of the Moon's craters were made by rocks flying through space. When the rocks crashed into the Moon, they made holes. One crater is over 960 km wide!

The far side

The far side of the Moon cannot be seen from anywhere on Earth. The same side of the Moon always faces Earth. This is because the Moon doesn't spin as it **orbits** Earth.

Some spaceships, carrying astronauts, have gone all the way around the Moon. They took pictures of the far side. It looks a lot like the side that faces Earth.

The far side of the Moon looks the same as the side that faces Earth.

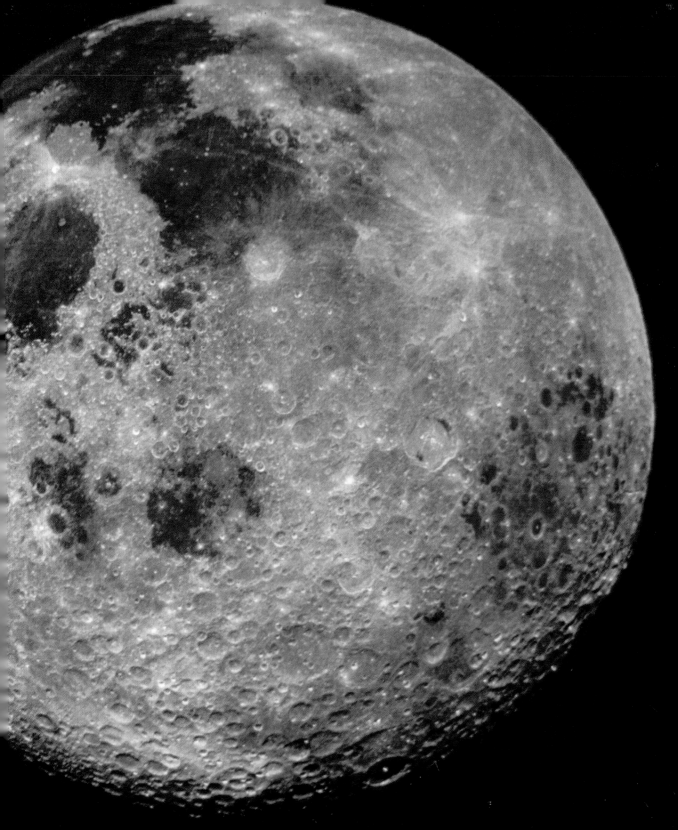

Tides

As the Moon travels around the Earth, it pulls on it. This pulling causes **tides**. When the Moon is over an ocean, the pull makes the water bulge. This water bulge is high tide.

When the Moon's pull on the ocean is strong, the tide is high.

When the Moon's pull on the ocean is weak, the tide is low.

As the Earth spins, the ocean moves away from the Moon and the pull is less. The water level falls. This is low tide.

Phases of the Moon

The Moon's different shapes are called phases.

The Moon has no light of its own even though from Earth it looks as if it does. In fact, the Sun's light is reflected off the Moon's surface. The Moon's **phases** are caused by the amount of sunlight that the Moon reflects.

It takes four weeks for the Moon to **orbit** the Earth.

As the Moon moves around Earth, it looks as if it changes its shape. It shrinks from a full moon to a thin **crescent**. Then it seems to disappear. But soon the Moon is back, growing bigger again.

Eclipses

Sometimes, the Moon moves between the Earth and the Sun. The Moon hides the Sun. This is called a solar eclipse. The sky gets very dark, even though it is daytime.

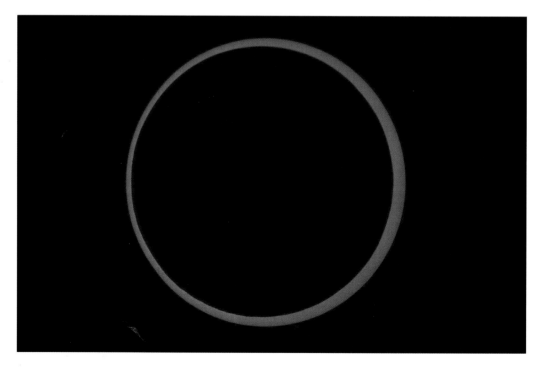

During a solar eclipse, the Moon hides the Sun.

In this picture, the Moon is only partly eclipsed. This means that only part of it is dark.

Sometimes, the Earth is between the Moon and the Sun. The Moon cannot reflect the sunlight so it goes dark. This is a lunar eclipse.

Never look right at the sun during an eclipse. The sunlight can hurt your eyes. It can even make you blind.

Visiting the Moon

For thousands of years, people could only look at the Moon from Earth. Then they built spaceships to explore space. On 20 July 1969, two astronauts called Neil Armstrong and Buzz Aldrin stepped onto the Moon.

Astronauts travel into space in rockets like this.

Buzz Aldrin walks on the Moon.

Neil Armstrong was the first of the two astronauts to step onto the Moon. He was followed by Buzz Aldrin. Since then, other astronauts have landed on the Moon.

Life on the Moon

There is no life on the Moon. The Moon has no air. It has little water. It is very hot on the side where it is lit by the Sun. The dark side of the Moon is much colder than any place on Earth.

Someday, people may try to live on the Moon. But they would have to bring air to breathe and food to eat. They would also have to wear special clothes to protect them from the very hot and very cold temperatures.

Someday, people may live and work on the Moon at a base like this one.

The Moon and everyday life

The Moon is important to us for many reasons:

- We get the word 'month' from the word 'moon'.
- The Moon causes **tides**.
- The movement of the high and low tides cleans our beaches.
- Tides can sometimes cause flooding during storms.
- The Moon reflects sunlight to give us some light at night.
- The Moon adds beauty to the night sky.

23

Glossary

craters holes made by objects such as rocks

crescent a shape that looks like a slice of lemon

orbit the path followed by the Moon

phase each different shape that the Moon appears to take

plains large areas of land that are very flat

planet one of nine huge ball-shaped objects that circle the Sun

satellite an object that circles around a larger object. The satellites of planets are called moons.

surface outside layers of something

tide the rise and fall of the surface of the sea

Index